For Matthew
—R.H.

For Nyima—who made this book possible
—B.B.

On this starry, starry night
the moon shines
its pale golden light.
Coyote howls
beneath the desert moon.
Who hears his lonely call
where cactus reach to the sky?

DISCOVER MY WORLD

Desert

Written by Ron Hirschi
Illustrated by Barbara Bash

A BANTAM LITTLE ROOSTER BOOK

NEW YORK · TORONTO · LONDON · SYDNEY · AUCKLAND

DESERT

A Bantam Little Rooster Book / September 1992

Little Rooster is a trademark of Bantam Books, a division of Bantam Doubleday Dell
Publishing Group, Inc.

Library of Congress Cataloging-in-Publication Data

Hirschi, Ron.
    Desert / by Ron Hirschi ; illustrated by Barbara Bash.
        p.   cm.—(Discover my world)
    "A Bantam little rooster book."
    Summary: Text and illustrations explore the variety of animal life
found in the desert.
    ISBN 0-553-08012-1.—ISBN 0-553-35497-3 (pbk.)
    1. Desert fauna—Juvenile literature. [1. Desert animals.]
I. Bash, Barbara, ill.   II. Title.   III. Series: Hirschi, Ron.
Discover my world.
QL116.H57   1992
591.909′54—dc20   91-14367
                                                            CIP
                                                            AC

Published simultaneously in the United States and Canada

PRINTED IN HONG KONG

0 9 8 7 6 5 4 3 2 1

Whooooo! Whooooo! Whooooooo!
Who am I,
flying on soft and silent wings,
calling when the coyote sings?

Do you see me jumping?
Quick! I must leave before
the owl hears me hurry.

Who am I
with ears alert
and antlers that look
like prickly cactus thorns?

And who am I,
searching for a meal,
tasting the air
with my tongue?

Who are we with glowing eyes,
following our mother
to the moonlit pool?

Who crawls through
the ooze and mud
where the spring waters soak
into the land?

And who trails its tail
across the driest desert sand?

Can you guess who hides
in its thick and sturdy shell?

As the sun rays touch
the cactus spines,
who follows the shadows
to a cool, daytime retreat?

Who creeps on many toes
across the sun-baked stones
and hot, hot sand?

Who runs on long legs
and searches for snakes?

And who followed
the swift roadrunner
to this resting rock,
shaded from the sun?
Was it a lone coyote,
or was it you?

 Coyotes call to one another in their own language and with a voice that is as much a part of the desert as the cactus and sand. They bark, yip, and whimper to communicate messages to family and to other coyotes.

 The feathers of a great horned owl are soft to help it fly silently. The edges of its wings break the wind with little or no sound. A hushed flight helps the owl sneak through night air to catch its prey.

 Kangaroo rats leap in a zigzag, ricocheting motion to confuse predators. As prey of many larger animals—such as coyotes, owls, and bobcats—these small mammals are an important part of the desert food chain.

 Mule deer antlers help to camouflage them and to keep them comfortable. When the wind blows, blood in the skin covering the antlers is cooled. This helps the deer survive in desert heat.

Desert Discoveries

 The rattlesnake's slender tongue is very sensitive and can taste tiny particles of scent in the air, helping it to seek out mice, birds, and lizards. Then it bites with a poisonous venom and swallows its prey.

 Raccoons hunt at night by using their keen senses of sight, smell, and touch. With their paws, they feel for frogs, fish, or snails in desert springs. Highly adaptable, desert-dwelling raccoons would feel at home in a city park.

 Spadefoot toads spend dry seasons buried in the sand, wrapped in a kind of toad jelly that may surround their bodies for as long as eight or nine months. When rain falls and creates a temporary pond, they emerge to sing and mate.

 Leopard lizards are one of many kinds of reptiles adapted to life in the desert. They scurry across the sand on their hind legs, trailing their tails as they run like miniature versions of Tyrannosaurus rex.

 Carrying their protective homes on their backs, tortoises burrow underground to avoid the hot sun. They may live for as long as fifty years if enough safe desert habitat is available for these slow-moving and vulnerable animals.

 Horns of the desert bighorn sheep grow larger each year and serve many purposes. Young males follow older sheep, who have large, curled horns and who know the way to summer feeding grounds.

 Active mainly at night, tarantulas slip out of daytime hiding places beneath stones or cracks in cactus and trees to attack insect prey. Like other spiders, they are often feared and unnecessarily harmed by people.

 Roadrunners have adapted to life on the ground. With their long, powerful legs, they can run faster than most birds, but they cannot fly as well as birds that spend more time in the air.